# BAPTIZED AND CONFIRMED

## Your Lifeline to Heaven

# BAPTIZED AND CONFIRMED
## Your Lifeline to Heaven

ELAINE CANNON

Visit us at www.deseretbook.com

ISBN 1-57345-915-1

First printed in hardcover in 1986.

Printed in the United States of America                                      54459-6786

10   9   8   7   6   5   4

# Table of Contents

*Place a picture of you*
*as a baby here.*

# A Word Before

No doubt about it, you are something wonderful.

As you prepare to be baptized and confirmed, use this book to help make the experience more special. To get started, paste in a picture of you as a baby. Later, add one taken on the day of your baptism and confirmation.

Look at the picture of you as a newborn—fresh from heaven. There was certainly a happy, heavenly spirit about you that day as family and friends crowded around. They were excited to get acquainted with you, and they were in awe. Each birth is a wondrous happening.

Before you were born, they talked about how you would look and what kind of talent would be fixed in your genes. They wondered if the life-shaping, eternal spirit assigned to the earthly body your mother and father had prepared was mellow or feisty.

And then you were born, a marvel of creation, with fingers to clench into fists, wiggling arms and legs, and facial features a mix of ancestors. Maybe you lucked out with a tousle of dark curls. And inside that soft bundle of baby joy was your very own spirit.

It is a God-given delight to be in the company of a brand-new person, whose spirit has just left the presence of Heavenly Father.

As you grew, you learned how to swallow your food, make noises, and form phrases with your mouth. You learned to grab, sit, crawl, walk, and get into mischief. Then you learned to use your head and become acquainted with an ever-expanding world outside yourself. It is now eight years later (or perhaps a few more, depending on your circumstances), and you are going to be baptized and confirmed. Already you are preparing to return to heaven.

Baptism is the first step back to the presence of Heavenly Father.

When you do return to his presence, many will be waiting to welcome you back from earth: Heavenly Father, ready to encircle you in the arms of his love; your elder Brother Jesus Christ; beloved people you called relatives on earth; friends and loved ones; prophets; and helpers in your life.

Being baptized and confirmed is your lifeline to heaven.

This book will help you understand that your life is made up of several spans:

1. *Premortal life*, which occurred before you came to earth, is where Heavenly Father created your spirit and where you became a child of God! While you were living in heaven in the premortal life, you were invited to a council in heaven, where Heavenly Father presented his plan of happiness and gave every spirit the agency to choose right or wrong. You were excited about going down to earth and receiving a physical body. In that council in heaven, your spirit person chose to follow Jesus Christ. Others, however, followed Satan, who was cast out of heaven because even then he did not obey Heavenly Father.

2. *Mortality* is where you are now, here on earth. It is in mortality that you learn and grow and come to understand what a body and a spirit are for.

3. *Immortality* will occur when you are resurrected. Your body and spirit will reunite after death, and you will

be able, if you have been obedient, to live with Heavenly Father again.

Remember always that Heavenly Father sent his spirit children to earth. He did not send us without rules to follow. He wants us back.

Being baptized and confirmed is the first step toward going back to heaven.

In this book you will learn what the two ordinances are and why they go together—you can't have one or do one without the other.

Because this is a new experience for you, there is a special section in the back of this book to tell you "What the Words Mean." If you see a word that is in bold, go to this section of the book and read about the word. There is also a special page near the end of the book for you to write about your baptism and confirmation.

Congratulations on this giant step! Your baptism and confirmation will provide you with a lifeline to heaven. With them, you'll definitely make it. Hang on tight and do what is right. Jesus will be your friend and helper. Get to know him. I know this is the plan of Heavenly Father for us. I know he lives and that Jesus is his Only Begotten Son who lived on earth.

Many hearty thanks go to Russell Orton, who first suggested I write this book. Thanks also to Cory Maxwell, who has been by my side during this project as a smart shepherd from start to finish. And, finally, thanks to beloved family members, true believers all. Some of them have already returned to heaven, and I am comforted that the steps were taken to lead them safely there.

# Chapter 1

# To You

Your **baptism** and **confirmation** are two of the most important things that will ever happen to you. They are your **lifelines** to heaven.

Jesus said, "Except a man be born of water and of the Spirit, he cannot enter into the kingdom of God" (John 3:5).

Jesus was baptized when he lived on earth. But his baptism was not for the **remission** of sins, as yours and mine are. Jesus was perfect—without sin. He was baptized because he wanted to be obedient to Heavenly Father's **commandments** and because he wanted to be an **example** for you and me.

When you are baptized by **immersion,** you are following Jesus. Being baptized and confirmed will be a most happy experience. It will be important to you forever. It can be helpful to you today and every day. It is a mark of personal progress. It is like being born again and given a new life. You will be washed clean.

Your baptism and confirmation will be public acts of your private **promises** with the Lord. You will never be the same again. Your soul, or your **spirit,** will seem full of light, filled with warmth, hope, and love. You will be given a **blessing** that is just for you, and you will know that. It will be wonderful.

After you have been baptized and confirmed, **Heavenly Father** will give you the **Holy Ghost** to help you always remember how you felt at that time—full of light and peace. When you pray to Heavenly Father, ask him to help you always remember.

Before you are laid down under the water in baptism and have hands placed upon your head in confirmation, you'll want to know more about the gospel. One of the **first principles of the gospel** is baptism. As you read about these things, you will begin to understand why this book is called *Baptized and Confirmed: Your Lifeline to Heaven*.

This book is especially for you as you prepare to be baptized and confirmed. I hope you find it fun to work with, interesting to read, and helpful too. It should remind you that Jesus loves you. The next chapter will tell you more about why Jesus loves you.

2

# Yes, Jesus Loves You

The beautiful cribs were ready. Mobiles of paper birds—red, yellow, orange, and blue, made by the children—floated one above each crib.

The diapers were folded and stacked. Ointments, oils, cotton balls, swabs—everything was ready.

Dad had gone to the hospital to get Mother and the brand-new twins. "Straight from heaven," explained Grandma, who had come to help. "With a portion of skill from Dr. Joki."

Twins! Wonderful!

They were beautiful, identical girl babies. No one could tell them apart. Mother had worked out a color system so that everyone would know who had been bathed and fed.

As the twins grew, each one was given the same care, the same food, the same tender love. They each slept in the same kind of crib in the same room. They rode face-to-face in a twin-size stroller. They were two of a kind, down to their soft baby hair, big eyes, and dimples.

Then, little by little, their differences began to show. For example, they were taught the same baby tricks, but there the sameness ended. Jane would pat-a-cake on request. Kristine would do it only when she wanted to. Jane loved to be taught. Kristine preferred to crawl off on a learning adventure of her own choosing, under the table, behind the couch, and into the pantry where Mother kept potatoes and cereal and other such fascinating items.

They were identical twins outside, but each had **unique** insides. The family loved both of them.

Two different eternal spirits had come from Heavenly Father to be housed in the twin bodies Mother and Dad had prepared for them.

What a discovery for the family!

And you too are a unique child. You are a child of God, like all of us, but you are special. Always have been. Always will be . . . you!

For the twins, for you, for me, for everyone, the start is the same: Long ago, in a world before this one, each of us received a spirit body as children of our Heavenly Father. Each person who has lived on earth— ever has or ever will—was spiritually **created** by Heavenly Father.

Can you think what that means?

It means that you, your mom and dad, your brothers and sisters, your grandparents, the bishop, your friends, your baby-sitter, and Jesus, too, are all brothers and sisters in the family of our Heavenly Father. Everybody on earth is related in this family connection.

Jesus was the first one born of our Father's spirit children. And he was the most obedient.

Jesus loves you.

You can read about that love in many, many places in your **scriptures.** You can hear about it in church. Most important, you can feel it in your heart.

Don't ever forget who you are. Your position is too wonderful for

4

that. Now when you sing that favorite song "I Am a Child of God," you will like it more than ever because you understand even better what it really means.

When you are baptized and then confirmed, your spirit will be **quickened,** and then you will be able to understand things about the world and yourself and Heavenly Father. Joyous things. You will come to understand how much Jesus loves you and why. As you learn more about Jesus and Heavenly Father, you will feel a deepening love for them. You will yearn to live with them through all **eternity.**

Jesus' mission to earth was a mission of love. He came to help every single one of us live forever—to gain back our physical bodies after death and then never die again. If it were not for Jesus' mission, this could never happen.

There is something else. You were born as part of a **master plan** for Heavenly Father's spirit children. Like the twins at the beginning of this chapter, you will keep growing and learning and helping while you are on this earth. After you die, your spirit will move forward to another stage of growth—first in the spirit world and then, if you have lived right, with your body returned to you and made glorious, in heaven.

5

This is the plan of God for us. You can read about it in your scriptures. Here are some good verses to start with: John 17:3; Mosiah 4:6–8; Moses 6:58–59; Abraham 3:24–26.

Because Jesus loves you, life is a great adventure, and **immortality** is a promise. Remember, under the direction of our Heavenly Father:

1. Jesus created the earth.
   All that is on it he created—
   stars, moon, sun,
   fruit and flowers and all growing things,
   animals, birds, and squiggly, wriggling creepers, too.

2. Jesus came to earth.
   He grew up strong, wise and good,
   teaching others,
   performing miracles,
   atoning for our sins.
   He was **crucified.**
   He was **resurrected.**

3. Jesus went back to heaven.
   He lives there now,
   and he leads, reveals, inspires
   his prophets and his people
   to help us get back to heaven.

You see, to get back to our Heavenly Father one day, what you have to do is follow your leader, Jesus Christ. See the next chapter about that.

6

# Chapter 3

# Follow the Leader

Follow the leader is an easy game to play: you simply do what the leader does.

Hilary was the leader in the game she was playing with her cousins. She marched like a soldier and danced like a ballerina, and Jenny, Katie, Catherine, Egan, Andrew, and Jake pranced along behind her. They did exactly what she did. They went wherever she led them. She did only good things. That was lucky, because they were good followers.

Their giggles sweetened the stifling hot air as the children skinnied between the meetinghouse and the wall that ran the length of the ditch behind the church property. Hilary led them around the wall to wade through the shallow ditch. Then up the bank they climbed, each one stopping in turn to toss a speckled stone into a puddle of water. They twisted their bodies, and each lifted up one knee in the same way Hilary did when she threw a stone.

Leaving the ditch, she led them hop-hop-hopping on one leg through a mint patch and past the columbine just bursting into bloom.

Suddenly Hilary dropped to her hands and knees. At once the children dropped to theirs. One by one they crawled past a chicken-wire fence, startling a mother hen. Quickly Hilary jumped to her feet and marched the group to the row of poplar trees edging the pasture. Hilary hugged each tree and whirled around it twice before moving on to the next smooth and cool, white-barked trunk.

Then they came to Grandmother's.

Hilary did three cartwheels and a somersault up the freshly mowed grass. Then the long lawn in front of Grandmother's house came alive with children whirling head over heels and rolling in every direction, like autumn leaves flung on the wind.

Hilary had many ideas about fun things to do and silly ways to move when playing follow the leader. It was never boring when she was their leader.

And when we understand correctly, it's never boring when Jesus is our leader. Of course, he doesn't lead us to do silly things like the ones children do when they are playing games. Those things are fun at a certain age, but we soon grow out of them. Jesus leads us in helpful ways, in important things that make growing up happy. There is no one better to follow.

8

When you are baptized and confirmed, you make a promise to follow him as exactly as you can. And because of Jesus' **atonement,** if you make a mistake, you can be forgiven.

Here are some of the things Jesus has taught. You can read about them in your own scriptures.

- If any man serve me, let him follow me (John 12:26).

- Wherefore [put] away lying, speak every man truth with his neighbor (Ephesians 4:25).

- Be ye kind one to another, tenderhearted, forgiving one another (Ephesians 4:32).

- Children, obey your parents in all things: for this is well pleasing unto the Lord (Colossians 3:20).

- Follow me, and do the things which ye have seen me do (2 Nephi 31:12).

- No unclean thing can enter into his kingdom. . . . Repent (3 Nephi 27:19–20).

- For all men must repent and be baptized, and not only men, but women and children who have arrived at the age of **accountability** (D&C 18:42).

- Draw near unto me, and I will draw near unto you (D&C 88:63).

- Remember the **covenant** wherewith ye have covenanted (D&C 90:24).

These are some of the eternal truths that Jesus taught.

When you follow your leader, as he has taught, then you are ready to be baptized and confirmed.

9

Are you ready? Or are there some things you may have done that you don't feel quite right about? The next chapter will help you learn what to do about them.

# Say You're Sorry!

Matthew was given a puppy for Christmas.

It was exactly what Matthew wanted. He had spent many nights snuggled in his bed thinking about how nice it would be if he had his very own puppy.

A puppy can be such a fine friend.

For a few days after Christmas, Matt took good care of Wiggles. That was the name he gave his puppy—Wiggles, because he wiggled!

Matthew put soft terry cloth in the bottom of the puppy's box. He even had his sister help him cover the box with bright contact paper. He measured the puppy food very carefully into the dog bowl. He checked the puppy's water bowl many times during the day to be sure his puppy wouldn't get thirsty. He loved Wiggles.

Then school started again after the holidays.

Matt got busy. He signed up for baseball after school, and with his friends he practiced tossing basketballs behind the school. He liked to read, and he was learning to play the bassoon, which took hours of practice.

And he forgot about Wiggles.

Not all the time, just some of the time. Mother reminded him and helped him, but he still kept forgetting.

And Wiggles was Matt's dog. He was Matt's responsibility.

Mother explained that she and Dad hadn't brought Matthew into the world and then left him, hoping someone else would feed and love him!

Matt said he understood.

But he forgot to feed Wiggles again. He said he was sorry.

The next time he forgot to feed Wiggles, he again said, "I'm sorry!"

He said it to Wiggles, and he said it to Mother, who was getting very impatient with Matt and his promises to take care of the dog.

One day Matt came home from school and said, "Wiggles. Here, Wiggles! Come on, boy. Come on."

Wiggles didn't come.

Matt called again. And again.

When the puppy still didn't come, Matthew went in the kitchen and asked his mother where Wiggles was.

"I have given him away."

"Given him away? Why?"

"You weren't taking care of him. You promised, but you didn't keep your promises, so I gave him to somebody who will take care of him."

"Mother! Wiggles is my dog! I *did* take care of him. I loved him. I fed him all the time."

"Matthew," said Mother slowly, "it has been days since I gave the puppy away, and you haven't even missed him."

"Oh!" Matthew hung his head thoughtfully. Then he lifted it to look into Mother's eyes. "How could you give him away?"

"I thought you didn't care about him."

"I am sorry I forgot to feed him, but I did care about him."

Mother said, "Matthew, when you say you are sorry, you are supposed to mean it. You promised you would take good care of him and you didn't, even when I reminded you."

Matthew began to cry.

Mother put her arm around Matt and pulled the crying boy to her. "You have a birthday next month, Matthew, and you will be eight years old. What happens then?"

"I'll get baptized."

13

Mother dried Matthew's tears and hugged him. "That's right. You'll make promises with Heavenly Father and Jesus. If you don't keep them, it will be much worse for you than forgetting to feed your puppy. And when you say you are sorry, you have to mean it. Do you understand? If you mean it and change your ways, you get another chance. Heavenly Father will **forgive** you. If you don't . . . well, it is more serious than having your puppy given to someone else. Don't forget this, Matt."

Saying you are sorry is part of what you do when you repent.

**Repentance** is feeling really, deeply sorry for something you have done wrong and making amends as much as you can. It also means not doing *wrong* again. Repentance is part of getting ready for baptism. But it's part of all the rest of your life too.

When you have broken one of Heavenly Father's commandments, you need to repent and ask him to forgive you. You also need to ask anyone else you may have offended to forgive you. Heavenly Father will expect you not to be disobedient anymore. If you do this, he will forgive you, and you will feel happy inside again. Repentance is changing your ways.

Some people think they can walk very close to sin and then just say, "I'm sorry," and that will take care of it.

They just don't understand. You need to understand that doing something wrong could never be right.

So when you've done something wrong, repent, say you are sorry, and then don't ever do that wrong thing again.

Stay far away from things that are wrong. Think of yourself as a tulip bulb, the kind your mom and dad bury deep in the earth during the fall months. They wait all winter long for the tulip to bloom. Finally, come springtime, beautiful colors fill their garden.

14

If, however, a bulb is not buried deep enough and is covered with just a little dirt, the bulb will freeze. The wind and rain and snow will cause the dirt to slip away. It will not survive the cold of winter, and it will never bloom. The bulb needs to be buried deep in the ground to remain warm and safe and to prepare to grow.

You too need to be buried deeply. You need to be buried deeply in the gospel, in doing things that are right, and in obeying your parents. Otherwise, the protection you receive from being obedient will quickly be washed away. You will be cold and exposed to great danger, just like the tulip that didn't survive the winter months.

You don't want to be close to sin. That simply makes no sense.

As you learn more about the gospel, you will see that the commandments are good. As you come to know Jesus and to love him, you will want to be more like him. You will want to try to match your life up to his. You will become a **disciple.** You will learn that Jesus gives good commandments that help you to be safe and protected deep in the "ground."

Jesus taught, "Ye must repent, and become as a little child, and be baptized in my name, or ye can in nowise . . . inherit the kingdom of God" (3 Nephi 11:37–38). You can read about this in your scriptures.

Only pure little children who have not reached the age of accountability do not need to repent and be baptized. Everyone else does. And even after we are baptized, we must be very careful or we will fall into traps set by **Satan.** That would be sad indeed.

Now that you understand the importance of repenting and telling Heavenly Father you are sorry, do you feel ready to be baptized and confirmed—to have **bestowed** upon you that special gift of the Holy Ghost to help you know right from wrong as you go through life? See what the next chapter tells you about this.

15

# Chapter 5

# Are You Ready?

Are you ready to be baptized and confirmed?

There are many things to think about when you are preparing for baptism. Getting ready takes more than setting the date. It is more than deciding to get baptized because some nice people have asked you to or because some of your friends are planning to be baptized and confirmed at the same time.

Baptism is a sacred **ordinance,** so you will want to be ready.

Think about these questions:

- Have you been taught the gospel?

- Have you learned the **Articles of Faith?**

- Do you pray?

- Do you want to be baptized and confirmed?

- Do you know what you are promising Jesus when you are baptized?

- Do you understand the difference this will make in your life?

- Are you ready?

As you find the answers to these questions, you will learn about yourself in this important, sacred step in your growth.

Of those who want to be baptized, the Lord has said: "All those who humble themselves before God, and desire to be baptized, and come forth with **broken hearts and contrite spirits,** and witness before the church that they have truly repented of all their sins, and are willing to take upon them the name of Jesus Christ, having a determination to serve him to the end, and truly manifest by their works that they have received of the Spirit of Christ unto the remission of their sins, shall be received by baptism into his church" (D&C 20:37).

To be ready for baptism, a person has to be at least eight years old and able to understand what the baptismal ordinance is. A person has to be mature enough to be able to choose to know and obey the gospel and make **covenants** with God. Children under the age of eight do not need baptism. They are not accountable. This scripture tells you why: "And their little children need no repentance, neither baptism. Behold, baptism is unto repentance to the fulfilling the commandments unto the remission of sins. But little children are alive in Christ" (Moroni 8:11–12).

Reviewing the following list will help you know whether you are ready to be baptized and confirmed:

1. Will you be at least eight years old at the time of your baptism?

2. Have you been taught the gospel of Jesus Christ?

3. Do you have **faith** in Heavenly Father and Jesus Christ?

4. Do you feel humble and needful before them?

5. Do you want to show other people, or be a **witness** to them, that you want to grow more and more like Jesus Christ?

6. Do you feel sorry about doing wrong things or giving in when you are **tempted?**

7. Have you repented, and have you told Heavenly Father how you feel and asked him to forgive you?

8. Are you willing to take on you the name of Jesus Christ and help him with his work?

9. Do you want to join his church on earth today—The Church of Jesus Christ of Latter-day Saints?

10. Are you familiar with the Articles of Faith of his church on earth today?

11. Do you and will you go to church regularly?

You ought to be able to answer yes to each of these questions. If you are in any doubt, speak to your parents about it. Or talk to your bishop or branch president. He will interview you for baptism anyway, and he will be interested in your preparations to be ready for this event.

And now—to be baptized!

# Baptized

Your baptismal day is a day of promise. It is a day of new beginnings.

Apart from being blessed and named (most likely as a baby), baptism is the first ordinance you will participate in as a child of God. Whether you are eight years of age or older, baptism is the first covenant you will make with the Lord. It prepares you for everything else the **priesthood** can bring to Church members—priesthood blessings, your **patriarchal blessing,** the **temple endowment,** temple marriage, and so on.

## Who

21

*Who takes part in your baptism?* You! And the person who baptizes you.

You will be at least eight years old and accountable, and you will have been taught enough about the gospel of Jesus Christ that you know that you want to be baptized.

The man who will baptize you will be one who holds the Melchizedek Priesthood or is a priest in the Aaronic Priesthood. There will be two witnesses, who will make sure that the ordinance is done as the Lord has said it must be. Maybe the person who baptizes you will be your father or your brother. Maybe it will be your home teacher. You will want to discuss this with the bishop or branch president.

Who else will be at your baptism? Perhaps all your family can be there. Your entire Primary class might want to come. You may invite anyone you would like to come to your baptism. Be sure to give them the time, date, and place.

# When

*When will you be baptized?* You and your bishop will set a date for your baptism. You have been learning about the gospel, and at age eight you are accountable before God. So you should not delay baptism. You should not delay your personal progress.

# Where

*Where will you be baptized?* A baptism is usually held at the stake center in the special baptismal **font.** But it might be done in a river, a lake, the ocean, or wherever there is clean water deep enough to immerse you completely. It is better if you are baptized in a place that is away from the busy world. This is the most sacred event you will have experienced in your life so far, and the surroundings should allow you to quietly think about it.

# What

*What happens at your baptism?* There will be a short program. A hymn will be sung. A talk will be given about this special ordinance that is going to take place. There will be a prayer.

At your baptismal service there probably will be others being baptized as well. You all will be dressed in clean white underwear and special heavy, white outer clothing. White clothing is worn as a symbol or sign of your personal purity, your worthiness to be baptized. If you have long hair, you may want to tie it in a ponytail to keep it from floating on the water. Remember, every part of you must be immersed.

After your baptism, you will dry yourself and dress in your Sunday clothes. (Don't forget to bring dry underwear.)

# How

*How will you be baptized?* The man who holds the priesthood and who will baptize you is someone you can trust. Before you are put down into the water, he will show you where to put your hands. He will show you how you can hold your nose when he lays you back under the water. In the actual baptism he will say the sacred words God wants said on this occasion. Then he will lower you into the water until you are all covered. You will be there for just a second or two. Then he will quickly raise you up again. The witnesses will watch carefully to see that all of you goes under. Your toe, a lock of hair, or a knee, for example, must not poke above the water. Remember to relax and let your body go under the water easily.

Getting baptized is exciting. It is not frightening. You will feel close to Jesus Christ. There is a good spirit at a baptism. Everyone there is happy—especially you.

23

The revelation given to the Prophet Joseph Smith instructing him how to baptize properly says: "The person who is called of God and has authority from Jesus Christ to baptize, shall go down into the water with the person who has presented himself or herself for baptism, and shall say, calling him or her by name: Having been commissioned of Jesus Christ, I baptize you in the name of the Father, and of the Son, and of the Holy Ghost. Amen" (D&C 20:73).

Some people in the world haven't learned about the true way to be baptized and what it really means to be baptized. They do not know that Jesus Christ set the example when he was baptized by immersion after the age of accountability.

In some churches, people are baptized by being sprinkled with water when they are babies. Other people are baptized when standing in a shallow pool while someone says a prayer. Some churches dip people into deep water but do not have God's authority or the proper prayer to baptize with. None of these ways is God's way. This is one of the reasons the LDS Church sends out missionaries—to teach people the true gospel and baptize them the right way with the right authority.

# Why

*Why are you baptized?* You are baptized because Jesus said you must be baptized in order to enter the kingdom of heaven. You see, only pure people can live in heaven with Heavenly Father. Baptism makes you spiritually pure; Heavenly Father forgives your sins. You have a fresh start. Going under the water washes you clean.

You are baptized because all of Heavenly Father's children who are accountable are invited to be baptized. Without that ordinance properly done, no one can get to heaven.

Adam, who was the first man on the earth, was baptized.

24

You can read about Adam's baptism in Moses 6:64–65. "When the Lord had spoken with Adam, our father, . . . Adam cried unto the Lord, and he was caught away by the Spirit of the Lord, and was carried down into the water, and was laid under the water, and was brought forth out of the water.

"And thus he was baptized, and the Spirit of God descended upon him, and thus he was born of the Spirit, and became quickened in the inner man."

Jesus was baptized.

Jesus was immersed in water. He walked down into the River Jordan with John the Baptist, who placed him under the water in baptism. He came forth as our example.

You can read about Jesus' baptism in Matthew 3:13–17.

The prophet Alma was baptized. You can read about Alma's baptism in Mosiah 18:10–14.

When you are baptized, you make a promise to Heavenly Father, and Heavenly Father makes a promise to you.

You promise that you will obey all of Heavenly Father's commandments.

Heavenly Father promises to forgive you when you repent from doing wrong. He also promises to let you come back and live with him forever after you are resurrected and have finished your time in earth life and in the spirit world. You will be very happy then. But while you are in this earth life, Heavenly Father promises you the gift of the Holy Ghost to help you through it.

The promise between you and Heavenly Father is called a covenant. It is a special kind of promise in that Father can only give you what he has promised if you keep your promise to keep his commandments.

It is important that you keep *all* promises you make. You do not want to fail others or hurt them in any way. Before you make any kind of promise you should consider its importance and how you will keep it. You should understand what is required of you.

That is one reason you have to be at least eight years old before you can be baptized—so that you will know what you are doing and what you are promising.

Abby's story will help you understand what keeping a promise is about:

Abby's mother asked her to go to the store and buy some ice cream for their family home evening.

"Abby," said her mother, "ice cream melts if it is out of the freezer too long. Please hurry right home with it after you buy it, will you? We want good ice cream for this special night. You may choose the flavor you like best, but promise me that you will come straight home."

"I promise," said Abby, nodding her head vigorously.

She meant it too. She was proud to have the chance to choose the ice cream for family home evening. It felt good that Mother trusted her to take the money and do the shopping. "I promise," she said again.

"Good girl," said Abby's mother. "Remember, the ice cream will melt if you stop and play." Her mother looked Abby right in the eye to be sure she understood the promise she was making.

"I know. Okay, Mother, and I'll hurry right home." And off she went to the store.

26

She bought mint chocolate chip. Just as Abby started out of the big doors of the grocery store, one of her friends came in. She asked Abby to go with her to the greeting cards rack. She wanted help choosing a birthday card for her father. "Help me choose, Abby, and then we can walk home together. It will be fun."

At first Abby agreed to help. It sounded nice to have a friend to walk home with. It wouldn't be boring that way. Choosing a card wouldn't take too long, either. She could get back in time.

Abby cradled the ice cream in her arm so that she could walk close beside her friend to the card rack. It was a good thing she shifted the ice cream. It felt cold against her arm. Suddenly Abby remembered that she had ice cream that wasn't supposed to melt.

She had promised Mother!

Abby explained to her friend and quickly said good-bye. She

hurried out of the door before she could change her mind or listen to her friend coax. And she ran straight home, her promise kept.

When you are baptized and confirmed, the Holy Ghost can remind you of promises you have made. He can help you know good from bad, truth from error.

You have to learn the signals. You have to learn how to listen and recognize the promptings of the Holy Ghost inside.

Abby kept her promise.

It is important for you to get in the good habit of keeping the promises you make with others—especially the promises you make with Heavenly Father and with Jesus.

It is easier to do what is right when you have made a habit of it.

Baptism is the first step on a ladder of promises that takes you to Heavenly Father.

27

Baptism is about promising, but it is about blessings too.

Heavenly Father asks us only to make promises that will be good for us, that will be helpful to us, and that will bring us special blessings. The gift of the Holy Ghost is one of the blessings you receive from Heavenly Father after baptism.

Being baptized and confirmed and receiving the Holy Ghost go together. The next chapter will tell you more about this.

# Chapter 7

# Confirmed

*Confirmed* is a word with a nice sound to it. At least, that is what Annie thought.

Ever since they had turned seven, Annie and Erin had talked a lot about getting baptized. They had helped each other memorize the Articles of Faith. They had whispered about feeling a little frightened about being put under the water. They had giggled about being wet in front of all the people. They had practiced holding their breath.

Being confirmed was different, though. You couldn't practice being confirmed.

They had a lot of questions about being confirmed. Maybe you have some, too. Here are some questions and answers that can help you understand more about this important happening following your baptism.

**Q.** What does it mean to be confirmed?

**A.** Confirmation is an ordinance in which the person is accepted into The Church of Jesus Christ of Latter-day Saints as a **member** and is given the gift of the Holy Ghost.

**Q.** When will I be confirmed?

**A.** Soon after you are baptized. It might happen as soon as you get dressed again after your baptism. It may not happen until the next fast and **testimony** meeting in your ward. You will work this out with your bishop.

**Q.** How is it done?

**A.** Men holding the Melchizedek Priesthood of God place their hands upon your head. You will probably sit on a chair in front of your family, friends, and members of your ward during the confirmation. You should close your eyes.

**Q.** What do these men say?

**A.** Speaking for all of them, one of the men will call you by your name and tell you that in the name of Jesus Christ and with the authority of the Melchizedek Priesthood, which they hold, they confirm you a member of The Church of Jesus Christ of Latter-day Saints. In the same manner, by "the **laying on of hands,**" they will bestow the gift of the Holy Ghost. It is a most sacred time in your life.

**Q.** What is the gift of the Holy Ghost?

**A.** It is the right to receive guidance from the Holy Ghost (Holy Spirit), the third member of the Godhead, as you live worthy of it and ask for it.

**Q.** What words are used to give me the gift of the Holy Ghost?

**A.** "Receive the Holy Ghost."

**Q.** What does that really mean?

**A.** It means that you are to take that gift from Heavenly Father—to receive it and use it. Have you ever given someone a gift that they put aside? Maybe they have even left it where it could become broken or spoiled. You won't want to do that with the gift of the Holy Ghost that your Heavenly Father gives you. The more you use that gift, the better it will become for you, and the more you will value the gift.

**Q.** What do I do with the gift of the Holy Ghost?

**A.** If you keep the commandments and pray to have the Holy Ghost as a companion, his influence will guide you. You will learn how to use this gift with wisdom as you grow up in the gospel.

**Q.** How long will I have this gift?

**A.** As long as you live on earth. But remember that to actually receive the Holy Ghost, to have his special influence, requires **obedience** and repentance. Repentance keeps you pure as you turn away from bad habits and temptations. Obedience makes you strong inside. It is then easier to do what Heavenly Father and Jesus want you to do.

**Q.** Why do we need the Holy Ghost? Why is life so hard?

**A.** Life is like a school. We are here to learn. We can't learn if everything is easy. When we have to think, reach, and try, we grow. Watch a baby learn to walk. Baby keeps trying, no matter how many falls he takes. How proud and happy that little person is when he is walking alone at last!

**Q.** How does it feel to have the Holy Ghost?

**A.** It feels good! When the Holy Ghost speaks to you as a **comforter** or a warning voice, you may hear a still whisper or a calm, firm command. You may feel a kind of burning in your heart. You may feel as if a warm cloak is about you. But don't worry, you will *know* when you have the Spirit with you. You will also know if that influence has left you. That will happen if you do something wrong and don't quickly repent of it or if you just don't bother to keep the commandments.

**Q.** How does this spirit or influence get inside of me?

**A.** We don't know, but Heavenly Father, who created us, does. He gives us the gift of the Holy Ghost to help us have a more full life. It

31

would be a good idea when you pray to thank Heavenly Father for this precious gift.

**Q.** How will I know when the Holy Ghost is trying to guide me?

**A.** You must listen carefully. You listen to the **still, small voice** that speaks to you in your mind and heart, to your **inner self.** When you listen to what the Holy Ghost tells you, when you follow his promptings, his warnings, or his comforting help, it will be good for you.

As an example, pretend that you are going on vacation to a strange new city. You don't know where to go or what to see. You don't really know the best way to use your time and money. So you buy a portable cassette player with headphones and a tape that will tell you where to go and explain all about what you will see when you get there.

32

Once there, with the tape player in hand, you will understand the interesting and beautiful experience more fully because you will have a personal guide speaking into your head through earphones. The tape will lead you through a maze of buildings, through crowds of strangers, and keep you from getting lost.

If you decide not to listen to the tape, however, you could get lost. You could miss seeing some of the best parts of the city.

The tape player is something like the spiritual guide Heavenly Father has given you to help you while you are here on earth, away from him. That guide is the Holy Ghost.

**Q.** Does the Holy Ghost have any other name?

**A.** Yes. Several. Names used when referring to the Holy Ghost include Comforter; still, small voice; teacher; prompter; Holy Spirit; and the Spirit.

**Q.** What is the Holy Ghost like?

**A.** The Holy Ghost is a personage of spirit. That is, he has a body shaped like a man's but made of spirit, which is invisible to our eyes. Though you cannot see him, you can feel his influence.

**Q.** Where can I find out more about the Holy Ghost?

**A.** There are many scriptures about the Holy Ghost. You can find them by looking in the Topical Guide of your Bible or the index of the Book of Mormon, the Doctrine and Covenants, and the Pearl of Great Price. For example, here are some scriptures that will be especially helpful and interesting to you as you get baptized and confirmed: Alma 34:38; Moroni 8:26; D&C 75:10–11; D&C 130:22–23.

**Q.** Who else has the gift of the Holy Ghost?

**A.** Only those people who have been baptized and confirmed members of The Church of Jesus Christ of Latter-day Saints are given the gift of the Holy Ghost. Of those, only people who keep the promises they made at baptism will actually receive the Holy Ghost. And out of that group, only those who keep their lives pure enough all the time will have the constant companionship of the Holy Ghost.

Now, aren't you glad about being baptized and confirmed?

Remember that you have a special calling and gift.

Remember to thank Heavenly Father for it.

Remember to listen to the promptings of the Holy Ghost. The next chapter will give you some suggestions on how to do this.

# The Gift of the Holy Ghost

Happy Birthday!

Merry Christmas!

Congratulations!

And a gift to mark the occasion.

A gift usually comes from someone who loves you and wants to be part of a special time in your life.

Your Father who is in heaven loves you too. When you are baptized and confirmed, he gives you a unique gift. It is the gift of the Holy Ghost. It will help you, if you will let it.

It helped Holly.

Holly loved the pine tree in front of her home. It towered so high above the house it caught summer breezes that cooled them before letting them ripple across the roof. It was almost like having an air conditioner.

That tree softened noise from the street close by. Its reaching base branches shaded Holly's favorite place to play. For sixty years pine needles had dropped to the ground below, forming layers of cushioning.

A blanket spread on this springy carpet softened the hard earth and kept the pine needles from pricking the bare legs of children who played there.

Holly had been baptized and confirmed. She was older than the children she played with. They looked to Holly as their leader. Often they would drag out boxes and blankets, books, pencils, and paper to play school. Sometimes Holly would read to them. She was a good reader. The words flowed so easily; it was as if she were just telling the story by heart.

One day there were three younger boys and girls listening to Holly read about Heidi, who also lived with her old grandfather by a big pine tree.

Suddenly a signal surfaced in her mind. Her heart started to thump as the command echoed in her head: "Move!" She responded at once. Scrambling to her feet, she shouted to the children to run. "Run!" She grabbed the smallest one by her arm, and the rest followed away from the pine tree. They thought it was a game—part of the story—until they heard a terrible crash.

A driver had lost control of his car on the road beyond. It had been going so fast that when it hit the curb, it jolted up and over the parking strip, the sidewalk, the lilac trees, and the boxwood bushes and flattened the garden stock. It hit against the big pine tree and stopped where the children had been playing only moments before.

Its engine still going, the car was wedged between the trunk of the tree and the huge limbs that flipped back into place after the impact.

The children were amazed. They stared at the car with its wheels spinning and its oil and gasoline sopping their blanket, their secret place. Some of the children were so frightened that they started to cry.

Holly didn't.

Holly was very, very quiet. She was thinking about the silent signal she had heard in her mind and heart that told her to move from the place under the tree. She suddenly knew that the warning had come to her from the Holy Ghost. The gift that she had received from Heavenly Father after she was baptized and confirmed had helped her just as she was promised.

That is how she knew she must move—by the signal inside of her from the Holy Ghost.

Like the other children, Holly still felt frightened as she stared at the upended car and the dazed driver inside. She knew now that she and the other children would have been badly hurt if they hadn't moved. But mostly she felt thankful for the help from the Holy Ghost. She decided that she would try always to listen to the quiet signals from the Spirit.

The Holy Ghost helped Emily too.

Every day Emily walked home from school with her friends past the park. There was a baseball diamond close to the corner. There were swings, slides, and bars for children.

Usually the little children had gone home from the playground by late afternoon when the big students came walking home from school or came to the park to play baseball.

This day the trees surrounding the sandlot of the playground were covered with fluffy pink and white blossoms. Emily thought they were beautiful. The girls stopped to count the trees. The afternoon sun was warm on their backs. The sky was blue and absolutely cloudless. Colorful crocuses popped through the park lawn.

It was a fine day. The girls felt alive. The park was quiet. They decided to swing like little children again. It would be fun.

So they did.

Soon the others left for their homes. Emily decided to stay for a while and swing longer. She loved it. It seemed so good to forget homework and not think about anything but just being carried right into the sky in the swing.

She pumped herself higher and higher. Then she let the swing sag toward earth, dangling her legs. Emily leaned her head against the thick chains for a moment, scuffing her feet in the sand to rest. Her cheeks still felt cool from the rush of the breeze during her swing.

Her thoughts were far away. A little song from Primary stirred her mind, "We do not have to see to know the wind is here; We do not have to see to know God's love is near. . . ."

Suddenly she felt the swing jolt. Someone had taken hold of the wooden seat she sat on. Someone had pulled her way, way back. Then she got a hard push that sent her soaring higher than she had ever been. Higher than she wanted to go. When she came back down she was caught again from behind, rudely. Again she was pushed. Hard.

Emily gripped the chains as the swing lifted high in the air. It was exciting, but it was scary, too. What a trick her friends had played on her to sneak back to the playground and frighten her! She didn't like it, really.

"Stop!" cried Emily.

A loud laugh was her answer. And then another push shoved her forward into the spring sky that only moments ago had seemed so lovely.

Emily clung to the chains and tried to look down at who was treating her to such a lively swing ride. She was dizzy, trying to see below the swing.

A young man stood there. He was not one of her friends. Emily had a strange feeling inside. He had control of her in that swing and she didn't even know him.

Then . . .

The swing was yanked to a stop. It jerked crazily. Suddenly the man's hands closed over hers on the chains, squeezing them together and then tightening her into his arms.

It was terrible. It was frightening.

She shivered.

Her heart began to pound.

Emily prayed to Heavenly Father silently while she wiggled as a captive.

And then—blessed answer. Her mind got the signal calm but firm: "Relax. Relax and don't fight. Then run!" Three times the command came.

Emily obeyed.

She let her body go limp. As Emily relaxed, the man loosened his grip on her. Immediately, she pulled her hands free from the chains. With her heart pounding, she ran.

She ran fast, out of the play area, around the picnic tables, away from the blossoming trees, picking up speed across the grass and away from the park.

She didn't look back.

That night as Emily knelt by her bed to pray, she felt safe and snug.

She remembered the signal that had come to her through the still, small voice while she was the stranger's captive in the swing.

She knew that Heavenly Father had answered her prayer. She knew that he loved her.

Emily was glad that she had obeyed. Her heart warmed as she thought about it.

Her prayers that night included thanks for such a gift.

Being confirmed after you are baptized brings many blessings into your life. Emily's experience is just one example.

Everyone who is baptized and confirmed in the Church has also been given the gift of the Holy Ghost. The person should then accept the gift. The Holy Ghost can work in a person's life only when he or she wants to have that help.

40

Also, the Holy Ghost can operate only when that person is clean and pure. The Lord has told us that "A [person] may receive the Holy Ghost, and it may descend upon him and *not tarry [stay] with him*" (D&C 130:23; emphasis added).

There are many gifts that we can enjoy because of the Holy Ghost. Find the following references in your scriptures: Luke 12:12; Moroni 10:8–19; D&C 46:11; D&C 121:26.

A most important thing is to learn to know when the Holy Ghost is speaking to you and understand what he is saying. As an example, let's talk about Nathan and José.

A new family moved next door to Nathan and his family. They had come all the way from Argentina. They said "sí" instead of "yes" and "gracias" instead of "thank you."

Nathan McOmber had fun playing with José Díaz. They were the same age, and José had learned to put the basketball through Nathan's hoop on the garage door on almost every throw.

The boys also taught each other different ways of saying the same thing. Sometimes they used sign language, drew pictures, or pointed to objects, and then said the word in their own language.

It was easier to communicate when they had learned more of each other's words. It also helped to listen very carefully when the other person was trying to teach.

Nathan liked José. He often prayed that Heavenly Father would help them understand each other.

The Spirit also speaks to us through a different language—the language of the Spirit—that we must learn to understand. It is the way the Holy Ghost tells us things.

41

It is good to learn how to listen to that language. It comes in your heart and in your mind.

Your parents and teachers have taught you that the Holy Ghost can warn you of danger, tell you things that you need to know, teach you, inspire you, help you to know right from wrong, and tell you about Heavenly Father and Jesus Christ. You know that these two beings are in heaven and that they care about you. The Holy Ghost witnesses this to you, inside, and you *know* it. That is one of the most important things the Holy Ghost does—he bears witness of the Father and the Son.

Getting baptized and confirmed and thus receiving the Holy Ghost brings you more blessings than you might have imagined. And you are only a beginner at understanding.

Some time after your baptism, you will think about it all again. It may be just before you drop off to sleep at night. It may be in the next fast and testimony meeting in your ward. Or it may be while you are writing a record of the event. Suddenly, a good feeling will warm your heart. You will know that Heavenly Father is near to you. You will feel that he is pleased with you.

That is comforting.

But what comes next?

What do you do after you are baptized and confirmed? The next chapter will give you some answers to that question.

# Chapter 9

# What Comes Next?

After you have been baptized and confirmed, you will be better able to tell right from wrong and know what truth is.

You will learn new things about how to live the way Jesus wants you to live—the way he lived.

You will want to please Heavenly Father. At first you may not always feel good about how well you are succeeding. But keep trying.

Compare yourself to an apple. Apples aren't bright, big, and ripe when they appear where blossoms used to be. Apples are hard, green lumps, at first.

Gradually apples grow. Gradually they become bright and big and ripe. And delicious.

Gradually people can become like Jesus too. Just as Briton and Benson were trying to do.

Briton and Benson and their family had been taught the gospel of Jesus Christ by the missionaries since Christmas. Each member of their family who was at least eight years old had been baptized that winter. Life seemed fine.

Until spring came.

When spring came, there were hard decisions to make. They were important decisions too. Such as what to do about Sundays.

Before they had been taught the gospel and were baptized, Sunday had always been a play day for the whole family.

Benson and Briton lived near a school ground where the junior soccer games took place. In fact, they went past the field every time they went to church. This particular day when they went by, the soccer field was bathed in sunshine. It was so bright outside that the sprinkler heads flashed like little mirrors hidden in the grass. And that grass was lush already, early for the season. The worn spots by the goalposts had even filled in. The spring sun had dried out the thawed earth. There would be no scruffing in the mud this day.

And what a day! It was the kind of day all of the teams had been waiting for. They had been waiting for it all winter.

The players were excited. They laughed and gently punched each other as they shimmied into their jerseys. It was maroon and blue against yellow and gray today. The field looked like an enormous patchwork quilt.

It also looked very inviting.

Briton and Benson saw all of this as they rode with their family past the field on their way to Sunday meetings at the church.

Last season both boys had starred in the championship games for the junior soccer title. Their team had finished in the top spot. Last year had been wrapped in glory for them. This year everything was different.

Their family had been baptized. No more Sunday soccer.

In their community the biggest game days were Sundays. Briton and Benson had joined the team for the workouts during the week, but when they told the coach they wouldn't play on Sundays, it had changed everything.

"Look guys," the coach scolded, "Sundays last all year. Soccer is only a short season. Go to your new church whenever you please but not on the Sundays of soccer season."

"Coach, you just don't understand," pleaded Briton.

"That's right, I don't. You play on Sunday with the rest of the team, or forget the whole thing. No exceptions. I have to treat every boy the same, Briton. You and Benson have to choose."

"We can play all the games but the Sunday ones," explained Benson. His heart was breaking. He was younger than Briton and hadn't had as much time in the game.

"You heard me," the coach said firmly. "No exceptions."

"Come on, coach. Please. Let up. Give us a chance."

"No way. It isn't fair to the others. Doesn't your church teach you about treating others as you'd like to be treated yourself or something like that? Well, the others on this team aren't asking for special treatment. Then neither should you, right?"

Coach thrust his hands into the pockets of his warm-up pants and stood staring at the boys with his legs spread apart. He looked like a giant. Strong. Immovable.

Briton and Benson looked at each other.

It was no use. They knew what they had to do.

When the family had decided to be baptized, they had talked about their new lifestyle. So no soccer on Sunday.

Suddenly the boys knew that the coach was right about no exceptions. No exceptions among the players or with the rules. But the

Church was right too. No exceptions. You belong; you make promises, so you live by the rules. That is what the family had talked about. If the choice had to be made between soccer on Sunday or pleasing the Lord, soccer lost.

The boys took their stand. They walked off the field.

"I'll give you twenty-four hours to change your minds," the coach called after them. "You'll always be welcome on my team. You are the best. We've trained you. We need you. Think it over."

The boys already had.

Now as they drove by in the family car on this bright Sunday, both Briton and Benson looked longingly at the action that had been part of their former lives. They stared out of the car window for as long as they could see the playing field, the colorful players, and the goal nets.

Even the two little ones were quiet in the car during the rest of the ride. Mom and Dad knew how the boys were feeling. Dad's voice was a little husky when he spoke to them.

"Hey! So what's soccer? It isn't the only thing in the world."

Nobody said anything.

Dad spoke again, clearing his throat. "Sons, your mother and I are more pleased with you today than we were a year ago when we clapped you off the playing field following the championship game."

"Naw," mumbled Benson.

"Yes, we are. You've made a grown-up decision. A tough, grown-up decision. And you were right. Soccer is fun, but it's just for now. Obeying your Heavenly Father is forever."

Their mother turned slowly around and smiled a small smile of encouragement toward the back seat where the boys were sitting.

"Mom. Dad. Don't worry about it." Briton brightened a bit and patted his dad's shoulder. "We all talked it over. We agreed to be baptized. It puts us on a different team, that's all. I just wish the coach had understood. But it's still okay."

And suddenly it was.

Briton and Benson were examples.

You can be an example.

When you have repented and been forgiven through baptism and have been given spiritual strength, what kind of life will you live? What comes next?

47

For one thing, you go on growing in the gospel. Each step opens another learning door. By now you probably enjoy finding help and direction on a subject through your scriptures. A fine scripture you can read is in Doctrine and Covenants 75:10–11:

"Calling on the name of the Lord for the Comforter, which shall teach them all things that are expedient, . . . praying always that they faint not."

See? You aren't alone anymore.

That makes all the difference. Being baptized and confirmed and being given the gift of the Holy Ghost mean that blessings come next. Obligations and opportunities come, too, because you are now a full member of The Church of Jesus Christ of Latter-day Saints.

Let's go over it again. What comes next after you have been baptized and confirmed?

You already know it means that your life will be somewhat different from the lives of many other people. And you will be glad it is.

Here is a Think List to help you remember what comes next:

1.  You have a fresh start.

2.  If you make a mistake, you can be forgiven if you repent and ask your Heavenly Father.

3.  The Holy Ghost will warn you of danger, whisper ideas, witness to your inner self that God lives and loves you, and help you know right from wrong.

4.  You take the **sacrament** each Sunday and remember the **sacrifice** of our Savior and think about the covenant you made by being baptized.

5.  You pay tithing. You will help the kingdom of God on earth grow by giving back to the Lord his tenth—one part in ten of everything you earn.

6.  You can get a recommend someday to receive a patriarchal blessing.

7.  You will learn to love people and help them because they are your brothers and sisters in Heavenly Father's family. You will try not to bring **contention** into the home. You will try not to be **covetous.**

8.  You will learn to give up some things in favor of better ones. Read about this in your scriptures in Doctrine and Covenants 89.

9.  You will be a better example of a person who has faith that Christ is his **Savior.** You can read about this in your scriptures.

48

Find 1 Timothy 4:12–14 in your Bible and 2 Nephi 31:5–10 in your Book of Mormon.

This chapter has been about what comes next. But what comes after "next"? It's *always remember*. We talk about that in the next chapter.

# Chapter 10

# Always Remember

It's easy to be good when everyone else is.

It's easy to be good when you are alone, on your knees, talking to Heavenly Father.

But often it is difficult to be what you want to be when you are out in the real world with people you don't understand, who don't understand you, and who don't seem to want to do what's right. But you can do it. You have all kinds of help.

Remember?

## You Promised:

- To take upon you the name of Christ. Read about it in Doctrine and Covenants 18:21–25.

- To bear one another's burdens that they might be light. Read about it in Mosiah 18:8.

- To stand as a witness of God at all times, in all things, and in all places, even until death. Read about it in Mosiah 18:9.

- To obey the commandments of God and to serve him. Read about it in Mosiah 18:10.

## God Promised:

- To accept each worthy person as a member of his Church and kingdom on this earth. Read about it in Doctrine and Covenants 20:37.

- To forgive your sins if you repent and ask God. Read about it in Doctrine and Covenants 58:42 and 33:11.

- To give you the gift of the Holy Ghost and to allow you your **agency** in actually receiving the Holy Ghost. You can choose to live your life with the marvelous help of this influence. Read about this in 2 Nephi 31:12.

- To bring you into the kingdom of God in heaven if you remain faithful and obedient for all of your earthly life. Read about this promise in 3 Nephi 11:33.

And that's what you want, isn't it, to go back to heaven and live forever with those you love?

52

Being baptized and confirmed is your lifeline to heaven; it is a key to **exaltation.**

Taking the sacrament every Sunday will help you always remember your baptismal promises and God's promises to you.

Remembering makes it easier to do what is right.

Now all of this calls for a celebration. The next chapter is about that.

# Chapter 11

# The Celebration

Being baptized and confirmed is a cause for joy. And that is another way of saying, "Let's celebrate."

The word *celebration* used to have a strictly religious meaning, but it has come to mean more often a time of festivity, of having a party, frequently of having noisy fun. Of course, that's not the right kind of activity when we celebrate a baptism. Being baptized and confirmed is a once-in-a-lifetime experience, and any celebration of it should be in keeping with the sacred ordinances.

Maybe your family will want to plan a special dinner in your honor. This ought not to be allowed to clash with the fast Sunday period, the weekend which is usually the time when baptisms and confirmations are held. Overfull stomachs don't help us have spiritual feelings. Fasting is spiritually strengthening.

You will be happy if you make a record of the event. You will make sacred promises and be given the gift of the Holy Ghost, so record your feelings.

Your personal journal is perhaps the best place to make this record. If you have not yet started one, maybe your parents or a relative will give you one for your eighth birthday. In this book you can fill in your name, date of baptism, and who baptized you.

Here are some other ideas that might help you mark the event.

- Get all the family in on planning your baptism if you can.

53

- Discuss what you want to do for the whole day as well as the details of the baptism itself.

- Ask yourself, Who is going to come? Where will you meet afterward? Do you want to give people invitations? Is the camera ready? (If you get to the baptismal service early enough you should be able to have a photo taken of you in your baptismal clothes, but that cannot be done while you are being baptized.)

- Wear your best clothes on your baptismal day.

- For your eighth birthday, ask for suitable gifts that others can give you in connection with your baptism. Good ideas include a copy of one of the scriptures: the Bible, the Book of Mormon, the Doctrine and Covenants, or the Pearl of Great Price. You might also like a book of remembrance with your name on it and your life details in it.

54

- Ask yourself if there is something memorable you'd like to make for the day. Maybe you'd like to have a white linen handkerchief that you could have embroidered with the date and place of your baptism. You could frame it and put it in your bedroom later. One family gives a brass key to the child getting baptized. It is something to remind him that baptism is the key to Heavenly Father's kingdom.

- Ask yourself if you want the day to be simple. If so, make sure it is kept that way. Make it your private time with the Lord, and that certainly will be celebration enough. You could have your father or mother read to you from the scriptures or from Church history (or your family history) some of the impressive stories of people in the past who have been baptized and found their happiness in their membership in the true church. (For examples, look in the Topical Guide in the LDS edition of the Bible under headings such as Baptism; Born; Conversion; Holy Ghost.)

# My Baptism

I was baptized on: _____ at _____ AM/PM

I was baptized by: _____

It was witnessed by: _____

My family and friends who came included: _____

_____

_____

_____

Place of my baptism: _____

My age at baptism: _____

My home address: _____

City: _____ State: _____

My ward: _____ My stake: _____

My bishop: _____

My thoughts on being baptized and confirmed: _____

_____

_____

_____

_____

_____

_____

_____

*Place a picture of you
from your baptism
day here.*

## Chapter 12

# To You from Me

When you are
baptized and confirmed,
people who love you
will get tears in their eyes.
Smiles will shine upon you.
Heavenly Father
will seem especially close.
You will feel
excited and warm inside.

Being baptized and confirmed
is like
having the whole yellow sun
where your heart
used to be.
It is being
filled with light.
To you
from me,
this is my testimony:

Heavenly Father
and Jesus Christ live.
They love us.
They have given
you and me
this time on earth.

They have given
you and me
principles to live by,
Church programs to grow through,
ordinances and promises
that have blessed my life
and can bless yours.
Life now
is preparation
for life after we die—
life in heaven with Jesus
and Heavenly Father.
Let us live
so that one day
we will all be there
with them
together.
Meanwhile,
learn of Jesus.
Follow him.
Help him.
And sometime
you will want
to bear your testimony
about how good you feel
about being
baptized and confirmed
because this is your
lifeline to heaven.

# The Articles of Faith

1. We believe in God, the Eternal Father, and in His Son, Jesus Christ, and in the Holy Ghost.

2. We believe that men will be punished for their own sins, and not for Adam's transgression.

3. We believe that through the Atonement of Christ, all mankind may be saved, by obedience to the laws and ordinances of the Gospel.

4. We believe that the first principles and ordinances of the Gospel are: first, Faith in the Lord Jesus Christ; second, Repentance; third, Baptism by immersion for the remission of sins; fourth, Laying on of hands for the gift of the Holy Ghost.

5. We believe that a man must be called of God, by prophecy, and by the laying on of hands by those who are in authority, to preach the Gospel and administer in the ordinances thereof.

6. We believe in the same organization that existed in the Primitive Church, namely, apostles, prophets, pastors, teachers, evangelists, and so forth.

7. We believe in the gift of tongues, prophecy, revelation, visions, healing, interpretation of tongues, and so forth.

8. We believe the Bible to be the word of God as far as it is translated correctly; we also believe the Book of Mormon to be the word of God.

9. We believe all that God has revealed, all that He does now reveal, and we believe that He will yet reveal many great and important things pertaining to the Kingdom of God.

10. We believe in the literal gathering of Israel and in the restoration of the Ten Tribes; that Zion (the New Jerusalem) will be built upon the American continent; that Christ will reign personally upon the earth; and, that the earth will be renewed and receive its paradisiacal glory.

11. We claim the privilege of worshiping Almighty God according to the dictates of our own conscience, and allow all men the same privilege, let them worship how, where, or what they may.

12. We believe in being subject to kings, presidents, rulers, and magistrates, in obeying, honoring, and sustaining the law.

13. We believe in being honest, true, chaste, benevolent, virtuous, and in doing good to all men; indeed, we may say that we follow the admonition of Paul—We believe all things, we hope all things, we have endured many things, and hope to be able to endure all things. If there is anything virtuous, lovely, or of good report or praiseworthy, we seek after these things.

# What the Words Mean

**Accountable:** answerable; in this case, having to answer to God for what we say and do. The Lord has told us that at age eight we become accountable and are able to choose baptism.

**Agency:** the God-given right each person has to make his or her own choice between good and evil.

**Articles of Faith:** thirteen statements written by Joseph Smith outlining the basic beliefs of The Church of Jesus Christ of Latter-day Saints. The Articles of Faith are included in the scriptures in the Pearl of Great Price.

**Atonement:** the great sacrifice Jesus Christ made when he took all the sins of mankind upon himself and made it possible for all of us to be resurrected. Atonement means that God and man have been brought together through Jesus Christ.

**Baptism:** a religious ceremony in which the person is laid under the water by a priesthood bearer for the remission of sins; *see also* Immersion.

**Bestowed:** given, like a gift, usually under special circumstances.

**Blessing:** special help from God, sometimes given through priesthood bearers as they lay their hands upon the person's head.

*Broken heart and contrite spirit:* a feeling of great awareness of one's wrongdoing. A deep sorrow for those sins and a willingness to repent and be obedient.

*Comforter:* another name for the Holy Ghost. On the day before he died, Jesus promised to send his disciples a Comforter to be with them while he was away from them. You can read about it in John 14:16, 26. Jesus Christ is also called the Comforter.

*Commandment:* something very important that God tells us to do. We will be blessed if we do what he says. We will be punished if we don't. Read about it in Doctrine and Covenants 130:20–21.

*Confess:* to admit or to tell God about wrong things we have done.

*Confirm:* to establish as true, make known; also to give a blessing following baptism that makes the person a member of the Church.

62

*Contention:* a quarrel or argument; also, an ill feeling that comes when people are not following the Savior's example of love.

*Covenant:* a sacred promise; an agreement between two or more persons that each will do certain things. Usually, a covenant is a two-way promise between you and the Lord.

*Covetous:* wishing or longing to have something that belongs to someone else.

*Create:* to start, build, or make from the beginning.

*Crucified:* killed by being nailed to a cross. Jesus was crucified.

*Disciple:* one who follows, especially a follower of Jesus.

*Eternity:* God's time. It has no beginning and no ending.

**Exaltation:** the highest level of life after death, where the righteous people will live in the presence of God.

**Example:** a model or pattern, in this case, of goodness.

**Faith:** total belief, in this case, conviction and trust in God the Father and in his Son, Jesus Christ.

**First principles of the gospel:** faith in Jesus Christ, repentance, baptism by immersion, and the laying on of hands for the gift of the Holy Ghost. See Article of Faith 4.

**Font:** a deep container used for special ceremonies, such as being filled with water for baptisms.

**Forgive:** to excuse or pardon; God forgives us when we have repented, then our sins are remitted, or wiped out, and God remembers them no more.

63

**Heavenly Father:** the Father of our spirits. We used to live in heaven with him. We hope to return to live with him again. We pray to him. He is also called God.

**Holy Ghost:** the third member of the Godhead, who works with God the Father and the Son Jesus Christ. He has power to help people on earth in special ways. He does not have a body of flesh and bone but has a spirit body. See D&C 130:22 and Article of Faith 1.

**Immersion:** being completely covered by water in baptism.

**Immortality:** living forever after dying in this life.

**Inner self:** the spirit created by Heavenly Father before the body was created by earthly parents.

**Laying on of hands:** a priesthood practice in certain ordinances and blessings. You can read about it in Mark 16:18.

*Lifeline:* something that allows you to survive or meet a great goal in life. The gift of the Holy Ghost is a lifeline because it gives answers and directions in times of trouble.

*Master plan:* the plan of salvation, a sacred plan, in which Jesus Christ created the earth and all that is on it. He did this under the direction of Heavenly Father. Then we were sent to this earth to each get a body. We learn, grow, and help Jesus in his work of bringing back to Heavenly Father all who will follow him. Read about it in Alma 42:5; Moses 1:39; Moses 6:62.

*Member:* one who is accepted as part of a group. You are baptized and then confirmed as a member of The Church of Jesus Christ of Latter-day Saints.

*Obedience:* doing what you are supposed to do when told by your parents, the law, or God.

64

*Ordinance:* a sacred ceremony carried out by a priesthood bearer, such as baptism, that will help you return to live with Heavenly Father again.

*Patriarchal blessing:* what God has to say to each of us about our mission on earth and the heritage we came from. This information is made known to us through the laying on of hands by a priesthood bearer who has been ordained a patriarch. This blessing is recorded in the Church archives.

*Priesthood:* the power of God acting through a properly ordained man.

*Promise:* a serious statement or agreement for certain behavior.

*Quickened:* kindled or fired up; made alive, full of energy.

*Remission:* forgiveness; baptism is for the remission of sins.

**Repent:** to feel sorrow for one's sins and forsake them.

**Resurrection:** the raising of the physical body from the grave and its being reunited forever with its spirit body.

**Sacrament:** an ordinance of the gospel of Jesus Christ. We take the sacrament of bread and water in remembrance of the flesh and blood of Jesus Christ, who sacrificed his life for us. Read about it in Moroni 4 and 5.

**Sacrifice:** to give up some desirable thing—such as one's life, as in the case of Jesus—especially for a belief.

**Satan:** a spirit child of Heavenly Father (as Jesus was and as we were), who was disobedient to Heavenly Father and was cast out of heaven. He lost his chance to have a body on earth, so he became angry, and ever since then he has tried to tempt people who have bodies. Satan is known by other names such as the adversary, Lucifer, the devil, and the evil one.

65

**Savior:** the Son of God, Jesus Christ. He was the Firstborn of Heavenly Father's spirit children and the only one ever to live a perfect life on this earth. The father of his earthly body was Heavenly Father. Mary was his mother. Because he was the Son of God in the flesh, he had the power to *not* die when he was crucified. He chose to die so that all people who ever come to earth might be saved after death. Because Jesus was resurrected, all people will be resurrected.

**Scriptures:** the word of God that he has revealed to his prophets; printed in four books: the Bible, the Book of Mormon, the Doctrine and Covenants, and the Pearl of Great Price.

**Spirit:** the part of you that was created by Heavenly Fahter in the premortal world. Your spirit is what makes you you!

**Still, small voice:** another name for the influence of the Holy

Ghost. Scriptures say that the voice of the Spirit is a still, small voice. It is not loud like thunder or an earthquake. It is quiet, but it can pierce your soul. It can make your heart "burn" and can be "heard" within you. It is so gentle that you might miss hearing it or not feel anything unless you are listening to or seeking help from Heavenly Father. Read about it in 1 Kings 19:12.

*Temple endowment:* a special ordinance performed in the temple. Like baptism, it is an ordinance in which you make promises that will help you return to live with Heavenly Father.

*Tempt:* to coax, persuade, entice; to make bad things look good and good things look bad. The devil tempts us to do things that will take us away from the Holy Spirit.

*Testimony:* a personal belief about Jesus and the gospel that the Holy Ghost tells us is true.

66

*Unique:* different from everyone or everything else in some way or ways.

*Witness:* a person who watches; for example, witnesses at your baptism see that every part of you goes under the water. Also one who bears a testimony of Jesus Christ and the gospel. After you have been washed clean through baptism, you can become a witness of the Lord Jesus Christ and his church.